POSITIVE
AND TE

G

TRANSFORM BEHAVIOUR WITH
BRAIN PATTERN INTERRUPTION

ISSI GISPAN

Positive Parenting and Teaching: Transform Behaviour with Brain Pattern Interruption
© Issi Gispan 2024

ISBN: 978-1-923197-59-6 (paperback)
         978-1-923197-64-0 (eBook)

A catalogue record for this book is available from the National Library of Australia

Printed in Australia by Ocean Reeve Publishing
www.oceanreevepublishing.com
Published by Issi Gispan and Ocean Reeve Publishing

REEVE
PUBLISHING

Contents

Introduction

The purpose of this book is to empower both educators and parents with practical tools and techniques necessary to positively influence the behaviour and emotional well-being of children and adults. We will explore methods that tap into the subconscious mind to create lasting positive changes. By understanding and utilizing the principles of brain pattern interruption and positive reinforcement, you will be able to foster healthier relationships, encourage desirable behaviours, and support personal growth. This approach is not only about correcting negative behaviours but also about nurturing and reinforcing positive ones, thus building a strong foundation for long-term development.

Understanding the Subconscious Mind

The subconscious mind operates below our level of conscious awareness, influencing our behaviours, thoughts, and emotions. It processes vast amounts of information without our conscious input, which is why habits and automatic responses are often driven by the subconscious. By directing positive suggestions to the subconscious, we can effectively alter these automatic behaviours. This e-book will guide you on how to communicate with the subconscious mind using specific techniques that bypass the analytical mind, leading to more profound and lasting behavioural changes. Techniques such as positive reinforcement and brain pattern interruption are particularly effective in this regard because they work by creating moments of receptivity within the subconscious mind.

Chapter 1

The Basics of Brain Pattern Interruption

What is Brain Pattern Interruption?

Brain pattern interruption is a powerful technique designed to disrupt habitual thought patterns, creating a moment of surprise or confusion. This disruption opens a window where individuals become more receptive to new suggestions because their subconscious mind, which usually operates defensively, becomes more alert and responsive. Rooted in Neuro-Linguistic Programming (NLP) and hypnotherapy, this technique leverages the brain's natural response to unexpected stimuli, offering a unique opportunity to introduce positive behavioural changes.

How It Works

At the core of this technique is the brain's reticular activating system (RAS), which filters and prioritizes information, helping us maintain focus. When an unexpected event occurs, the RAS immediately shifts attention to this new input, creating a brief period where the subconscious mind is highly receptive. This interruption of the usual thought flow induces a temporary state of confusion, during which the subconscious is more open to receiving and embedding new suggestions.

Example: In hypnotherapy, a sudden action like a handshake induction can briefly confuse the conscious mind, allowing the therapist to bypass normal thought processes and directly influence the subconscious. This surprise element interrupts the person's habitual thinking, making them more susceptible to the therapist's positive suggestions.

Benefits of Using This Technique

- **Increased Receptivity:** The element of surprise inherent in brain pattern interruption effectively captures attention, making the subconscious mind more open to new ideas. When the brain is caught off guard, it becomes more attentive and ready to absorb fresh information.

- **Reduced Resistance:** Disrupting expected patterns lowers defences making it easier to introduce and establish positive changes. The sudden shift in environment or interaction disrupts habitual responses, decreasing the likelihood of resistance.

- **Versatility:** Brain pattern interruption is a flexible technique that can be applied in various settings—classrooms, homes, therapy sessions, and workplaces. It is effective for both children and adults, making it a valuable tool for influencing behaviour in a wide range of contexts.

- **Quick Implementation:** One of the key advantages of brain pattern interruption is its simplicity and ease of use. These techniques can be quickly implemented in everyday situations without requiring extensive preparation, making them highly practical.

Practical Applications

- **In Education:** Educators can use brain pattern interruption to enhance classroom management and engagement. By introducing unexpected elements, teachers can capture students' attention, making lessons more interactive and effective.

  Example: A teacher might suddenly clap their hands or introduce a surprising fact to regain the attention of a distracted class, creating a moment of focus that enhances learning.

- **In Parenting:** Parents can leverage brain pattern interruption to manage their children's behaviour and strengthen relationships. By replacing expected reactions with positive, unexpected interactions, parents can redirect negative behaviours and reinforce positive ones.

  Example: Instead of scolding a child for misbehaviour, a parent might engage them in a fun activity, followed by a calm discussion of the behaviour, turning a potential conflict into a learning opportunity.

- **In Therapy:** Therapists can utilize brain pattern interruption to help clients break free from entrenched negative thought patterns, making them more receptive to positive changes. This technique is particularly useful in overcoming resistance to therapeutic suggestions.

  Example: A therapist might use a sudden shift in conversation or an unexpected question to disrupt a client's negative thinking pattern, facilitating a more open exploration of positive perspectives.

- **In the Workplace:** Leaders and managers can apply brain pattern interruption to improve team dynamics and foster a positive work environment. By breaking negative patterns, they can encourage creativity, collaboration, and motivation.

  Example: During a stressful project, a manager might unexpectedly call for a short, fun break, lightening the mood and boosting team morale.

Techniques for Brain Pattern Interruption

- **Physical Gestures:** Introducing an unexpected physical gesture, such as a light touch or sudden movement, can effectively interrupt thought patterns and capture attention.

  Example: A light tap on the shoulder during a heated argument can momentarily distract the person, providing an opportunity to redirect the conversation.

- **Changes in Tone:** Altering the tone of voice can create a surprising effect, making the listener more attentive and receptive.

  Example: Speaking in a calm, gentle tone during a tense situation can help defuse tension and open the listener to positive suggestions.

- **Unexpected Statements:** Using an unexpected statement or question can disrupt the usual flow of thoughts, creating a moment of surprise that primes the subconscious mind for new ideas.

Example: Asking an off topic but intriguing question during a monotonous discussion can re-engage the listener's attention, making them more open to new ideas.

- **Humorous Interventions:** Humour is a powerful tool for brain pattern interruption. A well-timed joke or playful comment can break tension, create a positive atmosphere, and make individuals more receptive to constructive suggestions.

  Example: A humorous observation during a stressful situation can lighten the mood and encourage a more positive and cooperative interaction.

Chapter 2

Positive Reinforcement and Its Power

Understanding Positive Reinforcement

Positive reinforcement is a behavioural technique that involves rewarding desired behaviours to strengthen and encourage their recurrence. This approach is based on operant conditioning, a principle in behavioural psychology suggesting that behaviours followed by positive outcomes are more likely to be repeated. By consistently rewarding positive actions, individuals are motivated to continue these behaviours, leading to long-term positive change.

How Positive Reinforcement Works

Positive reinforcement can be applied in various forms, such as verbal praise, tangible rewards, or additional privileges. The effectiveness of reinforcement depends on its immediacy and relevance. The closer the reinforcement follows the desired behaviour, the stronger the association between the action and the reward, thus making it more likely for the behaviour to be repeated.

Examples of Positive Reinforcement:

- **Verbal Praise:** Simple compliments like "Great job on your homework!" can significantly reinforce the behaviour of completing homework by making the individual feel recognized and appreciated.
- **Physical Rewards:** Tangible rewards, such as stickers, toys, or treats, can be used to reinforce desired behaviours, especially in children. For example, giving a child a sticker for cleaning their room reinforces the habit of maintaining cleanliness.
- **Additional Privileges:** Offering extra privileges, such as extended playtime or a special outing, can effectively reinforce positive actions. For instance, allowing a teenager extra screen time for completing tasks on time encourages responsibility and time management.

Long-term Benefits

- **Building Positive Habits:** Repeatedly rewarding positive behaviours helps in establishing and reinforcing good habits. As these behaviours are consistently rewarded, they become ingrained, forming a natural part of the individual's routine.

  Example: A child who receives praise and rewards for regularly brushing their teeth will develop the habit of maintaining good oral hygiene, which will likely continue into adulthood.

- **Boosting Self-Esteem:** Regular positive reinforcement enhances self-esteem and confidence, as individuals feel recognized and valued for their efforts. This sense of accomplishment encourages them to continue striving for success.

Example: An employee who consistently receives praise for their hard work will feel more confident in their abilities and motivated to maintain high performance levels.

- **Increasing Motivation:** Positive reinforcement is a powerful motivator. When individuals associate positive feelings with certain behaviours, they are more likely to continue those behaviours to experience those positive emotions again.

  Example: A student praised for participating in class will feel motivated to engage more, knowing their contributions are valued.

- **Improving Relationships:** Positive interactions foster trust and respect, which are the foundations of strong relationships. When individuals feel valued and recognized, they are more likely to develop positive connections with those providing the reinforcement.

  Example: A parent who consistently praises and rewards their child for good behaviour builds a stronger, more trusting relationship with their child.

Implementing Positive Reinforcement

- **Consistency is Key:** For positive reinforcement to be effective, it must be applied consistently. Reinforcement should be provided every time the desired behaviour occurs, especially in the initial stages, to solidify the connection between behaviour and reward.

Example: If a child is learning to clean up after themselves, consistent praise or rewards each time they do so reinforces the behaviour, making it a regular habit.

- **Immediate Reinforcement:** The reinforcement must closely follow the behaviour to strengthen the association between the two. Delayed reinforcement can weaken the connection and reduce its effectiveness.

  Example: Praising a child immediately after they complete their homework makes it clear that the homework completion is what earned the praise, reinforcing the behaviour.

- **Variety in Reinforcement:** Using a variety of reinforcement methods can keep the individual motivated and engaged. Mixing verbal praise, physical rewards, and additional privileges prevents the reinforcement from becoming predictable and less impactful.

  Example: Combining praise for effort with occasional small rewards like a favourite snack or extra playtime can maintain high levels of motivation.

- **Specific Praise:** When using verbal praise, it is important to be specific about the behaviour being reinforced. Specific praise helps individuals understand exactly what they did well, encouraging them to repeat that behaviour.

  Example: Instead of saying "Good job," say "Good job on solving that challenging math problem!" This specific feedback reinforces the effort and skill applied to the task.

Conclusion

Positive reinforcement is a powerful tool for encouraging desired behaviours and fostering long-term positive changes. By understanding how positive reinforcement works and implementing it effectively—through consistency, immediacy, variety, and specificity—individuals can build positive habits, boost self-esteem, increase motivation, and improve relationships. These long-term benefits contribute to creating a more positive and productive environment, whether at home, in the classroom, or in the workplace.

Chapter 3

Combining Positive Reinforcement with Brain Pattern Interruption

Introduction

The combination of positive reinforcement and brain pattern interruption creates a dynamic approach to influencing behaviour and promoting positive changes. By integrating these techniques, you can effectively capture attention, deliver impactful messages, and encourage desired behaviours. This chapter explores how these techniques can be combined to maximize their effectiveness in various settings.

The Protocol

Step 1: Create an Interruption

The first step in this protocol is to introduce an unexpected element that captures the person's attention. This interruption can be a physical gesture, a change in tone, or an unexpected statement. The goal is to momentarily disrupt the individual's current thought pattern, creating a receptive state for the upcoming positive message.

Examples:

- A gentle touch on the shoulder can surprise and capture attention, breaking the usual flow of thoughts.
- Clapping your hands softly can create a sudden, attention-grabbing sound, making the person more alert.
- Saying something out of context, such as "Look at that!" can redirect focus and prepare the mind to receive new information.

Step 2: Deliver the Positive Message

Once you have the person's attention, use a normal voice to convey a positive statement. This initial message sets a positive tone and creates a sense of security, making the individual more open to receiving the embedded suggestion that follows.

Example: "I love you," "You are doing a great job," or "I believe in you" are simple yet powerful statements that establish a positive atmosphere.

Step 3: Pause

Allow a moment for the positive message to sink in. This pause is crucial, as it gives the person's mind time to process the positive statement, creating a sense of anticipation for what comes next.

Example: After saying "I love you," pause to let the words resonate, enhancing their emotional impact.

Step 4: Whisper the Suggestion

In a lower tone or whisper, deliver the embedded command. This quieter tone signals to the subconscious mind that the message is important and should be internalized. The contrast between the normal voice and the whisper enhances the impact of the suggestion.

Example: Whisper, "And I know you can make better choices," "And I know you will sleep well tonight," or "And I know you're going to do a great job with your homework." This subtle shift in tone draws attention and reinforces the suggestion on a deeper, subconscious level.

Examples and Scripts

- **Behaviour Correction:**
  - ○ *Normal Voice:* "I love you."
  - ○ *Pause*
  - ○ *Whisper:* "And I know you can make better choices."

  Explanation: This script reassures the child of your love while gently encouraging them to make positive behaviour choices. The whisper adds emphasis, suggesting more likely to be internalized.

- **Bedtime Routine:**
  - ○ *Normal Voice:* "I love you."
  - ○ *Pause*
  - ○ *Whisper:* "And I know you will sleep well tonight."

  Explanation: This script uses positive reinforcement to create a calming bedtime routine. The whispered suggestion helps the child's subconscious mind accept the idea of a peaceful night's sleep.

- **Homework Time:**
  - ○ *Normal Voice:* "I love you."
  - ○ *Pause*
  - ○ *Whisper:* "And I know you're going to do a great job with your homework."

  Explanation: This script combines a positive message of love with a whispering suggestion that boosts the child's confidence and motivation to complete their homework successfully.

Tailoring the Scripts

These scripts can be tailored to fit specific situations and individual needs, ensuring that the message resonates with the person receiving it. Personalization enhances the effectiveness of the protocol, making it more relevant and impactful.

Examples:

- For a teenager struggling with self-esteem: "I love you. And I know you are amazing just the way you are."
- For an adult facing a challenging task: "You are capable. And I know you will handle this with grace and skill."

Integrating the Protocol into Daily Life

To maximize the benefits of combining positive reinforcement with brain pattern interruption, consider integrating this protocol into daily interactions. Consistency and repetition are key to reinforcing desired behaviours and creating lasting positive changes.

- **Morning Routine:** Start the day with a positive message and an encouraging whisper. For example, "Good morning, sunshine! And I know today is going to be a great day for you."
- **Mealtime Conversations:** Use mealtime as an opportunity to reinforce positive behaviours and attitudes. For instance, "You did great at school today. And I know you can keep up the good work."
- **Playtime:** Incorporate positive reinforcement during play to encourage cooperative and respectful behaviour. For example, "I love playing with you. And I know you can share your toys nicely."

Professional Settings

The protocol can also be adapted for use in professional settings, such as classrooms, therapy sessions, and workplace environments.

- **Classroom:** Teachers can use the protocol to encourage students and create a positive learning atmosphere. For example, "You are doing well on this assignment. And I know you can finish it with excellence."
- **Therapy Sessions:** Therapists can integrate the protocol to help clients internalize positive affirmations and suggestions. For example, "You are making progress. And I know you have the strength to overcome this challenge."
- **Workplace:** Managers can use the protocol to motivate employees and reinforce positive work behaviours. For example, "Your hard work is appreciated. And I know you will continue to excel."

Conclusion

Combining positive reinforcement with brain pattern interruption is a powerful technique for influencing behaviour and promoting positive changes. By following the steps outlined in this protocol and tailoring the scripts to fit specific situations, you can effectively capture attention, deliver impactful messages, and encourage desired behaviours in a compassionate and supportive manner. Integrating this approach into daily interactions can lead to lasting positive changes and improved relationships.

Chapter 4

Techniques for Educators

Classroom Management

Effective classroom management is essential for creating a productive learning environment. By integrating brain pattern interruption and positive reinforcement, educators can address disruptive behaviours while simultaneously encouraging positive ones. These techniques not only help manage the classroom but also foster a supportive atmosphere where students feel valued and motivated.

Examples and Applications

- **Example 1: Addressing Disruption**
    - **Scenario:** A student is being disruptive during a lesson.
    - **Technique:** The teacher walks over to the student, places a gentle hand on their shoulder, smiles, and says in a normal voice, "I love how creative you are." After a pause, the teacher whispers, "And I know you can use that creativity to focus on our lesson."

- Explanation: This approach surprises the student, shifting their focus and making them more receptive to the teacher's suggestion. The unexpected positive reinforcement captures their attention, reducing the disruptive behaviour and redirecting their energy towards the lesson.

- **Example 2: Promoting Engagement**
  - Scenario: A student seems disengaged and is not participating in class activities.
  - Technique: The teacher makes eye contact with the student and says, "I really appreciate your unique ideas." After a pause, the teacher whispers, "And I know you can share them with the class."
  - Explanation: By acknowledging the student's potential and encouraging them quietly, the teacher creates a moment of connection and receptivity. This can motivate the student to become more involved in class activities, fostering a more inclusive and dynamic learning environment.

Building Positive Relationships

Fostering trust and respect between teachers and students is crucial for a productive learning environment. Consistent positive reinforcement and genuine acknowledgment of students' efforts are key to building these positive relationships. When students feel valued and supported, they are more likely to engage actively in their learning.

Examples and Applications

- **Example 1: Regular Praise**
  - Scenario: A student completes a difficult project.
  - Technique: The teacher acknowledges the effort by saying, "I really appreciate how hard you're working on this

project," followed by a pause and a whispered, "You're doing a great job."

- ○ **Explanation:** This reinforcement not only recognizes the student's hard work but also builds their confidence. The combination of public praise and a personal whispered affirmation strengthens the teacher-student relationship, encouraging the student to continue putting in effort.

- • **Example 2: Encouraging Effort**
  - ○ **Scenario:** A student is trying to participate in class despite struggling with the material.
  - ○ **Technique:** The teacher can say, "I see how much effort you're putting into this," followed by a pause and a whispered, "Keep it up; you're improving every day."
  - ○ **Explanation:** Consistently recognizing and encouraging effort, regardless of the outcome, helps students feel valued and motivated to continue trying. This builds a supportive classroom environment where students feel safe to take risks and make mistakes.

Addressing Common Challenges

Educators often face challenges such as classroom disruption, lack of focus, and behavioural issues. By using brain pattern interruption and positive reinforcement, these challenges can be effectively managed, creating a more conducive learning environment.

Examples and Applications

- • **Challenge 1: Classroom Disruption**
  - ○ **Scenario:** A student is talking out of turn.
  - ○ **Technique:** The teacher gently touches the student's shoulder and says in a normal voice, "I appreciate your

enthusiasm." After a pause, the teacher whispers, "And I know you can share your ideas when it's your turn."

- ○ **Explanation:** This approach acknowledges the student's eagerness while subtly redirecting their behaviour. The physical touch and positive statement interrupt the disruptive pattern, and the whispered suggestion encourages the desired behaviour.

- **Challenge 2: Lack of Focus**
  - ○ **Scenario:** A student is distracted and not paying attention.
  - ○ **Technique:** The teacher walks over, makes eye contact, and says, "I love how much potential you have." After a pause, the teacher whispers, "And I know you can concentrate on this task."
  - ○ **Explanation:** Direct eye contact and a personal statement capture the student's attention. The positive reinforcement highlights the student's potential, and the whispered suggestion helps them refocus on the task at hand.

- **Challenge 3: Behavioural Issues**
  - ○ **Scenario:** A student frequently disrupts the class by getting out of their seat.
  - ○ **Technique:** The teacher approaches the student and says, "I notice you have a lot of energy." After a pause, the teacher whispers, "Let's use that energy to help with a special task."
  - ○ **Explanation:** This method acknowledges the student's energy and redirects it towards a positive activity. The unexpected task serves as a brain pattern interruption, while the responsibility given to the student acts as positive reinforcement.

Practical Tips for Educators

- **Consistency and Patience:**
  - ○ **Consistency:** Apply brain pattern interruption and positive reinforcement techniques consistently to reinforce desired behaviours. Consistency helps students understand expectations and feel secure in their learning environment.
  - ○ **Patience:** Be patient and give students time to adjust to these new techniques. Behavioural changes take time, and consistent application will lead to long-term benefits.
- **Tailoring Techniques:**
  - ○ **Personalization:** Tailor your approach to individual students' needs and personalities. What works for one student might not work for another, so be flexible and observant.
  - ○ **Feedback:** Encourage students to provide feedback on what techniques resonate with them. This collaborative approach can enhance the effectiveness of your methods.
- **Positive Classroom Environment:**
  - ○ **Positive Language:** Use positive language to create a supportive and encouraging atmosphere. Avoid focusing solely on negative behaviours; instead, highlight and reinforce positive actions.
  - ○ **Modelling:** Model the behaviours you wish to see in your students. Demonstrate respect, patience, and positivity in your interactions, setting a standard for students to emulate.
- **Continuous Learning:**
  - ○ **Professional Development:** Stay informed about new techniques and strategies in education. Attend workshops,

read relevant literature, and collaborate with colleagues to continuously improve your approach.

o **Reflective Practice:** Regularly reflect on your classroom management strategies and their effectiveness. Adjust your techniques based on your observations and student feedback.

Conclusion

Integrating brain pattern interruption and positive reinforcement into classroom management can transform the learning environment, making it more engaging, supportive, and conducive to positive behavioural changes. By understanding and applying these techniques, educators can address common challenges, build positive relationships, and create a foundation for long-term development and success for their students. This chapter provides practical strategies and examples that can be tailored to individual needs, empowering educators to foster a productive and positive classroom atmosphere.

Chapter 5

Techniques for Parents

At-Home Applications

Parents can use brain pattern interruption and positive reinforcement to address everyday challenges and create a positive home environment. These techniques can transform common parenting struggles into opportunities for building stronger relationships and encouraging desirable behaviours.

Examples and Applications

- **Example 1: Bedtime Resistance**
  - **Scenario:** A child resists going to bed, causing frustration for the parent.
  - **Technique:** Instead of getting frustrated, the parent can hug the child and say in a normal voice, "I love you." After a pause, the parent whispers, "And I know you will sleep well tonight."
  - **Explanation:** This unexpected, gentle approach captures the child's attention and makes them feel secure.

The combination of a loving statement and a quiet suggestion helps the child feel relaxed and more willing to cooperate with bedtime routines.

- **Example 2: Homework Struggles**
  - ○ **Scenario:** A child is reluctant to do their homework.
  - ○ **Technique:** The parent smiles, touches the child's shoulder, and says, "I love you." After a pause, the parent whispers, "And I know you're going to do a great job with your homework."
  - ○ **Explanation:** The positive reinforcement combined with a gentle touch and a quiet suggestion helps the child feel supported and encouraged. This approach reduces resistance and increases the child's motivation to complete their homework.

- **Example 3: Morning Routine**
  - ○ **Scenario:** A child is slow to get ready for school in the morning.
  - ○ **Technique:** The parent can cheerfully say, "I love how quickly you can get ready." After a pause, the parent whispers, "And I know today will be a great day for you."
  - ○ **Explanation:** This method uses positive reinforcement to create an expectation of quick and efficient behaviour. The quiet suggestion sets a positive tone for the day, making the child more cooperative and motivated in the morning.

- **Example 4: Sibling Conflict**
  - ○ **Scenario:** Children are arguing or fighting with each other.
  - ○ **Technique:** The parent can calmly separate the children, make eye contact, and say, "I love how well you

can get along." After a pause, the parent whispers, "And I know you can find a way to share."

- ○ **Explanation:** By focusing on the positive potential of the children, the parent redirects their behaviour towards cooperation. The whispered suggestion reinforces the expectation of sharing and resolving conflicts peacefully.

Strengthening Parent-Child Relationships

Building a positive and supportive home environment is key to effective parenting. By consistently using positive reinforcement, parents can acknowledge good behaviour, making children feel valued and recognized. This approach not only encourages desirable behaviours but also builds a trusting and loving relationship between parents and children.

Examples and Applications

- **Example 1: Consistent Praise**
  - ○ **Scenario:** A child shares their toys with a sibling.
  - ○ **Technique:** The parent says, "I'm so proud of you for sharing your toys." After a pause, the parent whispers, "You make everyone so happy when you share."
  - ○ **Explanation:** This positive reinforcement acknowledges the child's good behaviour and encourages them to repeat it. The whisper adds a personal touch, making the child feel even more appreciated.
- **Example 2: Encouraging Politeness**
  - ○ **Scenario:** A child uses polite language, such as saying "please" and "thank you."

- **Technique:** The parent says, "I love hearing you use such nice manners." After a pause, the parent whispers, "It makes me so proud."
- **Explanation:** By highlighting the child's polite behaviour, the parent reinforces the importance of manners. The whisper reinforces the personal pride the parent feels, encouraging the child to continue using polite language.

Addressing Common Challenges

Parents often face challenges such as bedtime resistance, homework struggles, morning routines, and sibling conflicts. By using brain pattern interruption and positive reinforcement, these challenges can be effectively managed, creating a more harmonious home environment.

Practical Applications

- **Challenge 1: Bedtime Resistance**
  - **Scenario:** A child resists going to bed.
  - **Technique:** The parent hugs the child and says in a normal voice, "I love you." After a pause, the parent whispers, "And I know you will sleep well tonight."
  - **Explanation:** This approach helps the child feel secure and more willing to cooperate with bedtime routines.
- **Challenge 2: Homework Struggles**
  - **Scenario:** A child is reluctant to do their homework.
  - **Technique:** The parent smiles, touches the child's shoulder, and says, "I love you." After a pause, the parent whispers, "And I know you're going to do a great job with your homework."

- **Explanation:** This technique reduces resistance and increases the child's motivation to complete their homework.
- **Challenge 3: Morning Routine**
    - **Scenario:** A child is slow to get ready for school.
    - **Technique:** The parent cheerfully says, "I love how quickly you can get ready." After a pause, the parent whispers, "And I know today will be a great day for you."
    - **Explanation:** This method sets a positive tone for the day, making the child more cooperative and motivated in the morning.
- **Challenge 4: Sibling Conflict**
    - **Scenario:** Children are arguing or fighting.
    - **Technique:** The parent calmly separates the children, makes eye contact, and says, "I love how well you can get along." After a pause, the parent whispers, "And I know you can find a way to share."
    - **Explanation:** This approach encourages cooperation and peaceful conflict resolution.

Success Stories

- **Success Story 1: Bedtime Routine**
    - **Scenario:** A parent struggling with their child's bedtime routine uses the technique of brain pattern interruption and positive reinforcement.
    - **Technique:** The parent hugs the child and says, "I love you," followed by a whispered, "And I know you will sleep well tonight."
    - **Result:** The child gradually becomes more cooperative at bedtime. Over a few weeks, the bedtime routine

becomes smoother, leading to a more peaceful evening for the entire family.

- ○ **Explanation:** The combination of a loving statement and a quiet suggestion helps the child feel relaxed and more willing to cooperate with bedtime routines.
- **Success Story 2: Homework Motivation**
  - ○ **Scenario:** A parent struggling to get their child to do homework uses the technique of brain pattern interruption and positive reinforcement.
  - ○ **Technique:** The parent smiles, touches the child's shoulder, and says, "I love you," followed by a whispered, "And I know you're going to do a great job with your homework."
  - ○ **Result:** The child becomes more motivated to complete their homework. Over time, homework time becomes less stressful and more productive.
  - ○ **Explanation:** The positive reinforcement combined with a gentle touch and a quiet suggestion helps the child feel supported and encouraged.
- **Success Story 3: Morning Routine**
  - ○ **Scenario:** A parent struggling with their child's morning routine uses the technique of brain pattern interruption and positive reinforcement.
  - ○ **Technique:** The parent cheerfully says, "I love how quickly you can get ready," followed by a whispered, "And I know today will be a great day for you."
  - ○ **Result:** The child becomes more cooperative and motivated in the morning. Over time, the morning routine becomes smoother and less stressful.
  - ○ **Explanation:** This method sets a positive tone for the day, making the child more cooperative and motivated in the morning.

- **Success Story 4: Sibling Conflict**
  - ○ **Scenario:** A parent struggling with sibling conflicts uses the technique of brain pattern interruption and positive reinforcement.
  - ○ **Technique:** The parent calmly separates the children, makes eye contact, and says, "I love how well you can get along," followed by a whispered, "And I know you can find a way to share."
  - ○ **Result:** The children become more cooperative and learn to resolve conflicts peacefully. Over time, sibling conflicts become less frequent and less intense.
  - ○ **Explanation:** This approach encourages cooperation and peaceful conflict resolution.

Conclusion

Integrating brain pattern interruption and positive reinforcement into everyday parenting can transform the home environment, making it more positive and supportive. By understanding and applying these techniques, parents can address common challenges, build strong relationships with their children, and create a foundation for long-term development and success. This chapter provides practical strategies and examples that can be tailored to individual needs, empowering parents to foster a positive and productive home atmosphere.

Chapter 6

Techniques for Special Situations

Dealing with Stress and Anxiety

Both children and adults can benefit from brain pattern interruption and positive reinforcement techniques to manage stress and anxiety. These methods provide immediate relief and long-term coping strategies by redirecting focus and encouraging positive actions.

Examples and Applications

- **Example 1: Test Anxiety**
  - ○ **Scenario:** A child is anxious about an upcoming test.
  - ○ **Technique:** A parent gently touches the child's shoulder and says in a normal voice, "I love you." After a pause, the parent whispers, "And I know you can take deep breaths to feel calm."

- **Explanation:** This approach helps the child focus on a positive action (deep breathing) to manage their anxiety. The unexpected gentle touch and positive reinforcement create a moment of receptivity, allowing the child to internalize the calming suggestion.
- **Example 2: Adult Stress Management**
  - **Scenario:** An adult is feeling overwhelmed by work-related stress.
  - **Technique:** A partner or friend can place a reassuring hand on the person's arm and say, "I believe in your ability to handle this." After a pause, they whisper, "And I know you can take a moment to breathe and relax."
  - **Explanation:** This technique uses positive reinforcement to acknowledge the person's capabilities while providing a simple, actionable step to manage stress. The quiet suggestion helps the person focus on breathing and relaxation.
- **Example 3: School-Related Anxiety**
  - **Scenario:** A child is anxious about going to school.
  - **Technique:** A parent hugs the child and says, "I know you're brave." After a pause, the parent whispers, "And I know you can have a good day at school."
  - **Explanation:** This method uses a loving statement and a quiet suggestion to build the child's confidence and reduce anxiety. The hug provides physical comfort, while the whispered reinforcement encourages a positive outlook.

Conflict Resolution

Using brain pattern interruption and positive reinforcement can effectively resolve conflicts by redirecting focus and encouraging cooperation. These techniques help create a calm and constructive environment for problem-solving.

Examples and Applications

- **Example 1: Sibling Arguments**
  - ○ **Scenario:** During a sibling argument, a parent intervenes.
  - ○ **Technique:** The parent places a hand on each child's shoulder and says, "I love you both." After a pause, the parent whispers, "And I know you can find a way to solve this together."
  - ○ **Explanation:** This approach surprises the children and redirects their focus toward cooperation and problem-solving. The physical touch and positive statement create a moment of receptivity, encouraging the children to work together to resolve their conflict.
- **Example 2: Peer Conflicts**
  - ○ **Scenario:** A teacher addresses a conflict between students in the classroom.
  - ○ **Technique:** The teacher stands between the students, makes eye contact, and says, "I appreciate how each of you can bring great ideas." After a pause, the teacher whispers, "And I know you can discuss this calmly and find a solution."
  - ○ **Explanation:** This technique uses positive reinforcement to acknowledge the students' potential for constructive discussion. The quiet suggestion encourages them to approach the conflict with a calm and cooperative attitude.

- **Example 3: Family Disagreements**
  - ○ **Scenario:** A disagreement arises during a family dinner.
  - ○ **Technique:** A family member intervenes by saying, "I love how we can all share our thoughts." After a pause, they whisper, "And I know we can listen to each other and understand different viewpoints."
  - ○ **Explanation:** This method redirects the focus from the disagreement to the positive aspects of sharing and listening. The whispered reinforcement encourages a respectful and understanding approach to resolving the conflict.

Encouraging Healthy Habits

Motivating positive lifestyle changes is another application of these techniques. By using brain pattern interruption and positive reinforcement, parents and educators can encourage healthy behaviors and habits in children and adults.

Examples and Applications

- **Example 1: Healthy Eating**
  - ○ **Scenario:** Encouraging a child to make healthy food choices.
  - ○ **Technique:** A parent says, "I love how you try new foods," followed by a pause and a whispered, "And I know you can make healthy choices."
  - ○ **Explanation:** This positive reinforcement acknowledges the child's willingness to try new foods and encourages them to continue making healthy choices. The quiet suggestion reinforces the behaviour in a supportive manner.

- **Example 2: Physical Activity**
  - ○ **Scenario:** Motivating a child to engage in physical activities.
  - ○ **Technique:** A parent says, "I love seeing you play outside," followed by a pause and a whispered, "And I know you can have so much fun being active."
  - ○ **Explanation:** This approach uses positive reinforcement to highlight the joy of physical activity. The whispered suggestion encourages the child to embrace an active lifestyle.
- **Example 3: Good Hygiene**
  - ○ **Scenario:** Encouraging a child to maintain good hygiene habits.
  - ○ **Technique:** A parent says, "I love how clean you keep yourself," followed by a pause and a whispered, "And I know you can keep up these great habits."
  - ○ **Explanation:** This method uses positive reinforcement to acknowledge the child's efforts in maintaining hygiene. The quiet suggestion reinforces the importance of continuing these habits.

Addressing Special Situations

Special situations, such as dealing with stress, resolving conflicts, and encouraging healthy habits, require tailored techniques to effectively manage and promote positive behaviour.

Practical Tips for Special Situations

- **Consistency and Routine**
  - ○ **Consistency:** Apply brain pattern interruption and positive reinforcement techniques consistently to reinforce

desired behaviours. Consistency helps individuals understand expectations and feel secure in their environment.

- ○ **Routine:** Establish routines that incorporate these techniques to create a stable and predictable environment.
This can help reduce anxiety and encourage positive
behaviour.
- **Personalization and Sensitivity**
- ○ **Personalization:** Tailor your approach to the individual's needs and personality. What works for one person
might not work for another, so be flexible and observant.
- ○ **Sensitivity:** Be sensitive to the individual's emotional
state and respond with empathy and understanding.
This helps build trust and encourages openness to the
techniques.
- **Positive Language and Modelling**
- ○ **Positive Language:** Use positive language to create a
supportive and encouraging atmosphere. Focus on reinforcing positive behaviours rather than solely addressing
negative ones.
- ○ **Modelling:** Demonstrate the behaviours you wish
to see in others. Show respect, patience, and positivity in your interactions, setting a standard for others
to follow.

Conclusion

Integrating brain pattern interruption and positive reinforcement into
special situations can transform how individuals manage stress, resolve
conflicts, and adopt healthy habits. By understanding and applying
these techniques, parents and educators can address unique challenges,
build strong relationships, and create a foundation for long-term

development and success. This chapter provides practical strategies and examples that can be tailored to individual needs, empowering parents and educators to foster a positive and productive environment for children and adults alike.

Chapter 7

Practical Tips and Tricks

Consistency and Patience

Consistency and patience are crucial when applying brain pattern interruption and positive reinforcement techniques. Consistency establishes
clear expectations, while patience ensures that behaviour changes are
reinforced over time.

Tips for Consistency and Patience

- **Tip 1: Stick to the Techniques**
    - **Description:** Regularly apply brain pattern inter-
    ruption and positive reinforcement techniques. Even if
    progress seems slow, continuing to use these methods
    consistently will eventually lead to positive outcomes.
    - **Example:** If a child is learning to put away their toys,
    consistently praise them every time they do it correctly.
    Over time, this will become a habit for the child.

- ○ **Explanation:** Consistency helps reinforce desired behaviours by making clear what is expected. Repetition strengthens the association between the behaviour and the positive outcome.
- • **Tip 2: Be Patient**
  - ○ **Description:** Understand that behaviour change takes time. Be patient and maintain a supportive attitude throughout the process.
  - ○ **Example:** When teaching a child to manage their emotions, patiently reinforce the techniques for calming down, even if it takes several attempts for the child to master them.
  - ○ **Explanation:** Patience is crucial because behaviour change does not happen overnight. Consistently applying positive reinforcement and brain pattern interruption will yield results over time, but it requires persistent effort and understanding.

Practical Applications

- • **Consistency in Daily Routines**
  - ○ **Scenario:** Establishing a morning routine for a child.
  - ○ **Technique:** Use positive reinforcement every morning when the child completes each step of the routine.
  - ○ **Example:** Praise the child for brushing their teeth and getting dressed on their own.
  - ○ **Explanation:** Consistent reinforcement helps the child understand and adhere to the routine, making it a natural part of their day.

- **Patience in Behavioural Changes**
  - ○ **Scenario:** Helping a child overcome bedtime resistance.
  - ○ **Technique:** Consistently apply the technique of a gentle hug and positive whisper every night.
  - ○ **Example:** Say, "I love you," followed by whispering, "And I know you will sleep well tonight," even if the child initially resists.
  - ○ **Explanation:** Patience ensures that the child feels supported and secure, eventually leading to a smoother bedtime routine.

Tailoring Techniques to Individual Needs

Personalizing techniques to fit individual needs enhances their effectiveness. Understanding each person's unique triggers and motivations allows for a more targeted and successful approach.

Tips for Tailoring Techniques

- **Tip 1: Understand Unique Triggers and Motivations**
  - ○ **Description:** Identify what motivates and encourages each person. Adapt your approach to suit their personality and preferences.
  - ○ **Example:** Some children may respond better to verbal praise, while others might prefer small rewards like stickers or extra playtime.
  - ○ **Explanation:** Personalizing techniques ensures that positive reinforcement and brain pattern interruption are most effective. By catering to individual preferences, you can more effectively encourage desired behaviours.

- **Tip 2: Adapt Your Approach**
  - ○ **Description:** Modify techniques based on the individual's needs and responses. Be flexible and willing to change your strategy if needed.
  - ○ **Example:** If a child is more motivated by extra playtime than verbal praise, use playtime as a reward for positive behaviour.
  - ○ **Explanation:** Tailoring your approach helps maintain the individual's interest and motivation, leading to better results.

Practical Applications

- **Adapting Techniques for Different Personalities**
  - ○ **Scenario:** Encouraging a shy child to participate in group activities.
  - ○ **Technique:** Use personalized positive reinforcement that suits the child's comfort level.
  - ○ **Example:** Praise the child for small steps, such as speaking up in a small group, and gradually build up to larger groups.
  - ○ **Explanation:** Tailoring reinforcement to the child's comfort level helps build confidence and encourages participation.
- **Understanding Triggers for Positive Behaviour**
  - ○ **Scenario:** Motivating a teenager to complete homework.
  - ○ **Technique:** Identify what rewards are most motivating for the teenager.
  - ○ **Example:** Offer additional screen time or a special outing as a reward for completing homework.

○ **Explanation:** Understanding what motivates the teenager ensures that the reinforcement is effective and encourages consistent positive behaviour.

Positive Reinforcement Strategies

Additional strategies for effective positive reinforcement include setting clear expectations and providing immediate feedback. These strategies help reinforce positive behaviours and ensure that individuals understand the connection between their actions and the positive outcomes.

Tips for Positive Reinforcement

- **Tip 1: Set Clear Expectations**
  - ○ **Description:** Clearly communicate what behaviours are expected and what the rewards will be.
  - ○ **Example:** Before starting a new chore routine, explain to the child what tasks they need to complete and what rewards they can earn.
  - ○ **Explanation:** Setting clear expectations helps individuals understand what is required of them and what they can achieve through positive behaviour.
- **Tip 2: Provide Immediate Feedback**
  - ○ **Description:** Give immediate feedback to reinforce positive behaviour. This helps individuals make the connection between their actions and the positive outcomes.
  - ○ **Example:** If a child completes their tasks, praise them right away and explain what they did well.
  - ○ **Explanation:** Immediate feedback reinforces the positive behaviour and helps the child understand the

connection between their actions and the positive reinforcement.

Practical Applications

- **Setting Clear Expectations in the Classroom**
  - ○ **Scenario:** A teacher wants to improve classroom behaviour.
  - ○ **Technique:** Clearly outline classroom rules and the rewards for following them.
  - ○ **Example:** Explain to students that completing assignments on time will earn them extra recess time.
  - ○ **Explanation:** Clear expectations help students understand what is expected and motivate them to follow the rules.
- **Providing Immediate Feedback at Home**
  - ○ **Scenario:** A parent wants to encourage their child to keep their room clean.
  - ○ **Technique:** Praise the child immediately after they tidy their room and explain what they did well.
  - ○ **Example:** Say, "Great job putting all your toys away! Your room looks so neat."
  - ○ **Explanation:** Immediate feedback reinforces the positive behaviour and helps the child understand the importance of keeping their room clean.

Conclusion

Consistency, patience, personalization, and effective positive reinforcement strategies are key to successfully applying brain pattern interruption and positive reinforcement techniques. By understanding and implementing these practical tips and tricks, parents and educators can create a supportive and encouraging environment that fosters positive behaviour and personal growth. This chapter provides actionable strategies that can be tailored to individual needs, empowering parents and educators to effectively influence behaviour and emotional well-being.

Chapter 8

Common Pitfalls and How to Avoid Them

Mistakes to Watch Out For

While brain pattern interruption and positive reinforcement techniques are powerful tools, there are common mistakes that can undermine their effectiveness. Understanding these pitfalls and how to avoid them can help ensure successful outcomes.

Mistake 1: Being Inconsistent with Reinforcement

- **Problem:** Inconsistency in reinforcement can confuse individuals and undermine the effectiveness of positive reinforcement.
- **Example:** Sometimes praising a child for good behaviour but ignoring it at other times.
- **Solution:** Maintain a regular pattern of positive reinforcement to build trust and reliability. Ensure that rewards and praise are given consistently for desired behaviours.

- **Example:** Every time a child completes their homework, they receive praise or a small reward.
- **Explanation:** Inconsistency can create confusion and uncertainty, making it difficult for the child to understand what behaviours are expected and rewarded. Consistent reinforcement helps to establish clear guidelines and promotes a sense of security and trust.

Mistake 2: Overemphasizing Rewards

- **Problem:** Relying too heavily on tangible rewards can lead to a dependence on these rewards rather than fostering intrinsic motivation.
- **Example:** Always giving a toy or treat for good behaviour instead of using praise or other forms of reinforcement.
- **Solution:** Balance tangible rewards with verbal praise and other forms of recognition that help build intrinsic motivation.
- **Example:** Praise the child's effort and dedication in addition to occasionally giving a small reward.
- **Explanation:** While rewards can be effective, it's important to also encourage children to develop internal satisfaction from their achievements. This balanced approach helps children learn to value their own efforts and accomplishments.

Mistake 3: Ignoring the Importance of Timing

- **Problem:** Delaying reinforcement can weaken the connection between the behaviour and the reward.
- **Example:** Waiting until the end of the day to praise a child for something they did in the morning.
- **Solution:** Provide immediate reinforcement to strengthen the association between the behaviour and the positive outcome.

- **Example:** Praise the child immediately after they complete a desired behaviour, such as cleaning up their toys.
- **Explanation:** Immediate feedback is crucial for reinforcing positive behaviour because it helps the child make a direct connection between their actions and the positive reinforcement. This immediacy enhances the learning process and makes the reinforcement more effective.

Maintaining Authenticity

The importance of being genuine and authentic in applying brain pattern interruption and positive reinforcement techniques cannot be overstated. Authenticity enhances the effectiveness of these techniques by building trust and credibility.

Tips for Maintaining Authenticity

- **Tip 1: Ensure Sincerity and Specificity**
  - **Problem:** Generic or insincere praise can come across as disingenuous and may not effectively reinforce the desired behaviour.
  - **Example:** Using generic phrases like "Good job" without specifying what was done well.
  - **Solution:** Provide specific feedback that is sincere and directly related to the individual's actions.
  - **Example:** "I really appreciate how you helped clean up your toys without being asked. You showed great responsibility."
  - **Explanation:** Authenticity is important because it reinforces the sincerity of the positive reinforcement. Specific feedback helps the individual understand exactly what behaviour is being praised, making it more likely

that they will repeat the behaviour in the future. Genuine praise fosters a deeper connection and more meaningful reinforcement.

- **Tip 2: Personalize the Reinforcement**
  - **Problem:** Using a one-size-fits-all approach to reinforcement can be less effective for individuals with different needs and preferences.
  - **Example:** Giving the same type of praise or reward to all children, regardless of their unique personalities.
  - **Solution:** Tailor the reinforcement to the individual's preferences and needs to make it more meaningful and effective.
  - **Example:** For a child who values verbal praise, emphasize specific compliments, while for another who prefers tangible rewards, occasionally incorporate small treats or privileges.
  - **Explanation:** Personalizing reinforcement makes it more impactful and relevant to the individual. Understanding what motivates and resonates with each person ensures that the positive reinforcement is effective and appreciated.

Practical Applications

- **Consistent Reinforcement in Daily Routines**
  - **Scenario:** Encouraging daily tasks.
  - **Technique:** Provide immediate and consistent praise every time the child completes a chore.
  - **Example:** "Great job setting the table! You did it so quickly and neatly."
  - **Explanation:** Consistent and immediate reinforcement helps solidify the habit of completing tasks.

- **Authentic Praise in the Classroom**
  - ○ **Scenario:** Recognizing student effort.
  - ○ **Technique:** Give specific and genuine feedback on student work.
  - ○ **Example:** "I was really impressed with the way you solved that math problem. You showed great problem-solving skills."
  - ○ **Explanation:** Specific praise helps students understand what they did well and encourages them to continue putting in effort.
- **Personalized Reinforcement at Home**
  - ○ **Scenario:** Motivating a child to practice a musical instrument.
  - ○ **Technique:** Combine specific verbal praise with occasional tangible rewards that the child values.
  - ○ **Example:** "I loved hearing you play that new piece on the piano. You've improved so much! How about we celebrate with some extra playtime?"
  - ○ **Explanation:** Personalized reinforcement that acknowledges the child's specific achievements and preferences is more motivating and effective.

Conclusion

Avoiding common pitfalls in applying brain pattern interruption and positive reinforcement techniques is crucial for their success. Consistency, authenticity, and personalization are key factors that enhance the effectiveness of these techniques. By understanding these common mistakes and implementing practical solutions, parents and educators can create a supportive and encouraging environment that fosters positive behaviour and personal growth. This chapter provides actionable strategies to help avoid these pitfalls and ensure successful outcomes in influencing behaviour and emotional well-being.

Chapter 9

Measuring Success

Tracking Progress

Measuring the success of brain pattern interruption and positive reinforcement techniques is essential to ensure their effectiveness and to make necessary adjustments. Tracking progress provides valuable insights into behaviour changes and helps reinforce positive behaviours by recognizing and acknowledging improvements over time.

Methods for Tracking Behaviour Changes and Progress

- **Tip 1: Keep a Journal**
  - **Description:** Maintain a journal to record specific instances of positive behaviour and any changes observed over time.
  - **Example:** Note down behaviours like "Completed homework without reminders" or "Handled a conflict calmly."
  - **Explanation:** A journal helps track progress and identify patterns in behaviour. It allows for detailed documentation of what techniques were used and their

outcomes, providing a comprehensive overview of the child's development.

- **Tip 2: Use Behaviour Charts**
  - ○ **Description:** Create behaviour charts to visually monitor improvements and track specific behaviours.
  - ○ **Example:** Use a chart with columns for the date, behaviour, positive reinforcement given, and notes on progress.
  - ○ **Explanation:** Behaviour charts offer a clear and visual representation of progress, making it easier to see trends and patterns. They can be a motivating tool for children, as they can see their achievements over time.
- **Tip 3: Regular Check-ins**
  - ○ **Description:** Schedule regular check-ins to review progress and discuss any challenges or successes.
  - ○ **Example:** Weekly or bi-weekly meetings with children or students to talk about their behaviour and progress.
  - ○ **Explanation:** Regular check-ins provide an opportunity for feedback and discussion, allowing for timely adjustments to techniques and reinforcement methods.

Practical Applications

- **Behaviour Journals at Home**
  - ○ **Scenario:** Tracking a child's progress in managing emotions.
  - ○ **Technique:** Parents can write daily entries noting instances where the child managed their emotions well and what reinforcement was given.
  - ○ **Example:** "Today Jamie used deep breathing to calm down after getting upset. Gave praise and extra playtime as a reward."

- Explanation: This method helps parents see how often and under what circumstances the child is successfully managing their emotions, providing insights into which techniques are most effective.

- **Behaviour Charts in the Classroom**
  - **Scenario:** Monitoring student behaviour and participation.
  - **Technique:** Teachers can use behaviour charts to track positive behaviours such as participation, cooperation, and task completion.
  - **Example:** A chart with categories like "Participated in class discussion" and "Helped a classmate," with stickers or marks to indicate each instance.
  - **Explanation:** Visual charts help students understand their progress and motivate them to continue exhibiting positive behaviours.

Adjusting Techniques as Needed

Flexibility and responsiveness to feedback are crucial for refining and adjusting techniques to ensure they remain effective. Everyone is unique, and what works for one person may not work for another.

How to Refine and Adjust Techniques Based on Results

- **Tip 1: Be Flexible and Responsive to Feedback**
  - **Description:** Pay attention to feedback and be willing to modify your approach if a particular technique isn't working.
  - **Example:** If verbal praise isn't motivating a child, switch to a small reward system.

- Explanation: Flexibility ensures that techniques are adapted to meet the individual's needs and preferences, increasing their effectiveness.
- **Tip 2: Experiment with Different Methods**
  - Description: Try various techniques to see which ones are most effective for the individual.
  - Example: Combine verbal praise with tangible rewards or alternate between different types of positive reinforcement.
  - Explanation: Experimentation helps identify the most effective methods and allows for a more tailored approach to behaviour management.
- **Tip 3: Continuous Improvement**
  - Description: Regularly review and assess the effectiveness of the techniques being used and adjust as needed.
  - Example: Use the data from behaviour charts and journals to refine strategies.
  - Explanation: Continuous improvement ensures that the techniques remain relevant and effective over time, adapting to the individual's changing needs.

Practical Applications

- **Adapting Techniques for Different Age Groups**
  - Scenario: Tailoring reinforcement techniques for different age groups.
  - Technique: Use age-appropriate rewards and methods of reinforcement.
  - Example: Younger children may respond better to stickers and small toys, while older children might prefer extra screen time or privileges.

- ○ **Explanation:** Age-appropriate techniques ensure that reinforcement is meaningful and motivating for the individual.
- • **Using Feedback to Improve Techniques**
  - ○ **Scenario:** A student is not responding well to verbal praise.
  - ○ **Technique:** Switch to a tangible reward system and observe the changes.
  - ○ **Example:** Provide a small reward like extra recess time for positive behaviour and track the student's response.
  - ○ **Explanation:** Using feedback to adjust techniques helps find the most effective methods for reinforcing positive behaviour.

Conclusion

Summarizing Key Points

Positive reinforcement and brain pattern interruption are powerful tools for promoting positive behaviour change. Consistency, patience, and authenticity are key to their success. These techniques can be applied in various settings and tailored to individual needs to achieve lasting positive outcomes.

- • **Summary:**
  - ○ **Consistency:** Regularly apply techniques to reinforce desired behaviours.
  - ○ **Patience:** Allow time for behaviour changes to take effect.
  - ○ **Authenticity:** Provide sincere and specific reinforcement.
  - ○ **Tailoring:** Customize techniques to individual needs and preferences.

- o **Explanation:** These key points emphasize the importance of using these techniques consistently and authentically, and the need to tailor them to the individual to achieve the best results.

Encouragement and Next Steps

- **Encouragement:** Believe in the power of these techniques and your ability to make a positive impact. Continue learning and adapting to improve your approach. Small, consistent efforts can lead to significant changes over time.
  - o **Explanation:** Encouraging words help to motivate and inspire educators and parents to implement these techniques and continue to develop their skills in promoting positive behaviour change.

Appendices

Resources and Further Reading

Additional resources, books, and articles for further learning:

- **List:**
  - "The Power of Positive Parenting" by Glenn Latham
  - "Positive Discipline" by Jane Nelsen
  - Online courses and workshops on behaviour management and positive reinforcement techniques.
  - **Explanation:** Providing additional resources helps to support further learning and development, allowing educators and parents to deepen their understanding and refine their techniques.

Templates and Worksheets

Practical templates and worksheets to help implement the techniques:

- **Templates:**
  - Behaviour charts
  - Progress tracking sheets

- ○ Script templates for positive reinforcement and brain pattern interruption
- ○ **Example:** A behaviour chart can include columns for the date, specific behaviour, positive reinforcement given, and any notes on progress.
- ○ **Explanation:** Practical tools and resources help to facilitate the implementation of the techniques, making it easier for educators and parents to track progress and reinforce positive behaviours.

By following the guidance provided in this e-book, educators and parents can effectively apply brain pattern interruption and positive reinforcement techniques to foster positive behaviour changes and support the emotional well-being of children and adults. The strategies and resources offered will help create a nurturing and encouraging environment that promotes personal growth and development.

Milton Keynes UK
Ingram Content Group UK Ltd.
UKHW022012131124
451149UK00013B/1116

9 781923 197596